Contemporary Asian Americans

MAYA LIN

BY
BETTINA LING

RSVP
**RAINTREE
STECK-VAUGHN**
P U B L I S H E R S
The Steck-Vaughn Company

Austin, Texas

Published by Raintree Steck-Vaughn, an imprint of Steck-Vaughn Company.
Produced by Mega-Books, Inc.
Design and Art Direction by Michaelis/Carpelis Design Associates.
Cover photo: ©Adam Stoltman 1989

Library of Congress Cataloging-in-Publication Data
Ling, Bettina.
    Maya Lin/ by Bettina Ling.
        p. cm. — (Contemporary Asian Americans)
    Includes bibliographical references (p. 47) and index.
    Summary: Describes the life and work of the Chinese-American architect who designed the Vietnam Veterans Memorial in Washington, D.C., and the Civil Rights Memorial in Montgomery, Alabama.
        ISBN 0-8172-3992-8 (Hardcover)
        ISBN 0-8172-6881-2 (Softcover)
    1. Lin, Maya Ying—Juvenile literature.
2. Chinese-American architect—Biography—Juvenile literature.
[1. Lin, Maya Ying.   2. Architects.   3. Sculptors.
4. Chinese Americans—Biography.   5. Women—Biography.]
I. Title. II. Series.
NA737. L48L56 1997
720' .92—dc20   96-45935
[B]   CIP
                                                                  AC

Printed and bound in the United States.

1 2 3 4 5 6 7 8 9 LB 00 99 98 97 96

Photo credits: ©Uniphoto Picture Agency/Roddy Mims: p. 4; AP/Wide World Photos: pp. 7, 23, 32; UPI/Corbis-Bettmann: pp. 8, 18, 28; ©Margaret Miller/Photo Researchers, Inc.: p. 11, ©Mark C. Burnett/Photo Researchers, Inc.: p.12; ©Thomas S. England/Photo Researchers, Inc.: p.31; ©Renate Hiller/Monkmeyer: p. 15; ©Richard Vogel/Gamma-Liaison: p. 17; ©Earl Young/Archive Photos: p. 20; Courtesy of Juniata College: p. 24; ©Topham/The Image Works: p. 27; Courtesy of Charlotte Coliseum: p. 35; Courtesy of Michael Marsland/Yale University Office of Public Affairs: p. 36; ©Beryl Goldberg: p. 39; Courtesy of Darnell Lautt/Wexner Center, The Ohio State University: p. 40; Bob Kalmbach/The University of Michigan: p. 43; ©1992 Richard Howard/Black Star: p.44.

Contents

Chapter One

ARCHITECT
OF HISTORY

She won! Shocked and surprised, Maya Lin hung up the telephone in her dorm room at Yale University in New Haven, Connecticut. It was May 1981, and Maya was a 21-year-old student. She had just received the news from Washington, D.C., that her entry in an important design contest had been chosen by the judging committee.

A national competition had been held to find a design for a **memorial** honoring the men and women who had served and died in the Vietnam War. This war had caused a lot of debate in America during the 1960s, when the United States sent troops to help the South Vietnamese people fight against the North Vietnamese Communists. The United States continued to send

Maya Lin won the largest design competition in the United States, while still a student at Yale University.

armed forces until 1973, and many American soldiers died in the war.

Americans had been very divided over the United States's involvement in this war. A lot of Americans felt we were helping the South Vietnamese fight against **Communism**. But just as many Americans thought our country had no right taking part in another country's war. Years after the war had ended, Americans were still bitterly at odds about it. And the soldiers who fought and died in Vietnam had never been properly honored for their service and bravery.

In the late 1970s, a man named Jan Scruggs came up with the idea to build a memorial to these soldiers. Jan believed a memorial would serve two purposes: It would heal the bitterness still felt by many Americans, and it would honor those who had fought and died in the war. He talked to other Vietnam veterans about a memorial, and many of them also thought it was a good idea. So Jan and some other veterans formed the Vietnam Veterans Memorial Fund.

A site for the memorial was picked in Washington, D.C., between the Lincoln Memorial and the Capitol. A national competition was held to find a design for the memorial. It was the largest design contest ever held in the United States.

Maya Lin's proposal for the memorial had been selected as the winning entry. She would receive $20,000 in prize money, and her design would become a part of American history. Maya could not

Jan Scruggs, head of the Vietnam Veterans Memorial, speaks at a convention of Vietnam Veterans in Washington, D.C.

believe her good fortune. She had never really expected to win. She was studying architecture, the art and science of designing buildings and other large structures. Her entry had begun as a class assignment for one of her college architecture courses. Her professor had urged her to enter the design in the competition. There were thousands of entries, most of them from famous and experienced architects, designers, and artists. Even Maya's professor had entered the competition. Surely one of those professionals would win, Maya thought. She was a senior in college, and she'd received only a B as the grade for her design in her architecture class. But the phone call from the memorial fund committee was official. Maya Lin's entry was selected as the one to be used for the memorial!

Maya's winning design would mark the beginning

Maya Lin's design for the Vietnam Veterans Memorial was selected from thousands of entries, including one from her own architecture professor at Yale University. Here she displays the model of her final design.

of a brilliant career in architecture and art. Before the age of 35, she would create some of the most significant public **monuments** and works of art in the United States.

Her talent and achievements have already brought her a number of awards, including a Presidential Design Award, memberships in two Women's Halls of Fame, and honors from *Time* and *Life* magazines and the American Institute of Architects.

But all of this was to come after designing a very important historical memorial. Here was an opportunity of a lifetime for someone so young, who wanted a career in art and architecture. Little did Maya know that her work on the Vietnam Veterans War Memorial would be one of the greatest and most difficult challenges of her life.

Chapter Two

A FAMILY
OF ARTISTS

Maya Ying Lin grew up in the small college town of Athens, Ohio. Athens is tucked away in the hills of southeast Ohio, an area of the Midwest that is dominated by rivers, lakes, and woods.

Athens is also the home of Ohio University, and the brick streets of the town hum with the energy of the students. There are many craft stores, art galleries, and studios that reflect the region's strong artistic tradition. The combination of the small scholarly town and the beautiful rural country setting made Athens "the perfect place to grow up," says Maya.

Maya was born in Athens, on October 5, 1959. Her parents were Chinese immigrants (people who move to another country to live permanently). Maya's mother, Julia Chang Lin, was born in Shanghai, China. Her father, Henry Huan Lin, came from a very distinguished family of anti-Communist politicians and thinkers in Beijing, China.

Henry and Julia Lin fled China right before the Communists took over the country in 1949. The Lins came to America and settled in Athens, where both became professors at Ohio University. Henry Lin eventually became the university's dean of fine arts. He was a ceramist, an artist who makes objects such as earthenware (pottery), porcelain, or tiles from fired clay. His ceramic artwork filled the Lin home. Growing up surrounded by her father's work had a deep influence on Maya.

As a child Maya experimented with many different artistic techniques, including ceramics. Her father taught her how to make pots and sculpture out of clay. The young Maya would often beg her father to let her "throw" a pot. "Throwing" means to form a lump of wet clay into the shape of a pot with your hands, as the clay turns on a spinning cylinder, called a potter's wheel.

Maya's mother, Julia Lin, was and still is a professor of English and Oriental literature at Ohio University. A published poet and author, Julia Lin also had a strong artistic influence on her daughter. Maya's home life was a place of art and literature. Her family had a great respect for creativity, and her parents encouraged Maya and her older brother, Tan, in their artistic pursuits. Maya loved to read, especially fantasy books, such as Tolkien's *The Hobbit*. Although Maya spent most of her time with her family or playing by herself, she and Tan also had fun playing

Maya Lin's father, Henry Huan Lin, was dean of fine arts at Ohio University. A ceramist like the woman in this photo, he inspired Maya to become an artist.

long games of chess together, or with some of the other children in the neighborhood.

Throughout her childhood Maya made things using many different art forms. Besides ceramics Maya also experimented with silversmithing (making objects out of silver) and bronze casting (making sculptures out of bronze metal). She liked to make jewelry and create both small and large sculptural figures. And she says she spent hours by herself building little towns in her room.

Since the Lin family lived in a rural, wooded area of forests and hills, Maya often took long walks and

Maya Lin has always found inspiration in nature. This photo shows the Ohio Indian Mound, built by the Adena Culture. Sometimes it is called the "Great Serpent Mound," because it looks like a giant serpent uncoiling.

hikes in the woods near her home. She grew to love and respect nature. These feelings would influence Maya's future work in art and architecture. Nature is a theme in most of her designs, and she has a deep commitment to preserving the environment. Maya says that she always "hopes [her] work will be sensitive to the environment, working with it, instead of trying to conquer nature or command it."

Maya really loved school and studying. In high school she was a good student but a bit of a loner.

Maya wore no makeup and didn't really date. She did particularly well in mathematics and was interested in biology, the environment, and the study of animals. Maya took some college courses while she was in high school, too. At her graduation in 1976, Maya was the co-valedictorian (a person who shares the highest grade average in a graduating class) of her high school class.

Maya applied and was accepted to Yale University. During her first year of college, Maya took sculpture classes and explored other areas of the arts. She discovered that in the field of architecture, the design and construction of buildings and other structures required knowledge of engineering, mathematics, and art. Realizing she had found an area of the arts that would combine both her love of science and art, Maya began studying architecture in addition to her other art classes.

Three

"THE WALL"

At Yale Maya worked hard in her art classes at the School of Fine Arts and on her architecture projects at the School of Architecture. During her undergraduate years at Yale, Maya was once told by her professors that she could be either an architect or an artist, but that she couldn't be both. Maya never believed that to be true. She was not interested just in sculpture and crafts but also in clothing and furniture design and portrait photography. So besides studying subjects related to her major in architecture, Maya continued to take sculpture and art classes. As far as Maya was concerned, she would always consider herself both an architect and an artist.

During her junior year, the Yale School of Architecture offered Maya the opportunity to study in Denmark for a semester. While there Maya visited other cities in Europe and became interested in the cemetery architecture she saw. Because many

European cities are tightly packed with buildings and have little land space left, the graveyards are often also used as public gardens where people go to walk or sit. Maya found this idea of cemeteries serving as both burial places and as gardens for the living very interesting. After returning from Europe, Maya wanted to learn more about this subject.

Her senior year Maya decided to take a course in burial (funerary) architecture taught by Professor Andrus Burr. The Vietnam Veterans Memorial design competition was announced during the period Maya was taking this class. Professor Burr gave his class the assignment to create a design for the memorial.

Maya Lin's design for the Vietnam Veterans Memorial was influenced by the architecture found in cemeteries. Maya realized that cemeteries are as much for the living as they are for those who have died.

The Vietnam Veterans Memorial design competition had certain rules for designing the memorial. The four most important rules were: It had to contain the names of all persons who were killed or missing in action in the Vietnam War; it could not make a political statement about the war; it had to be a quiet place for people to think and reflect on what happened in the war; and it had to be in harmony with its location and the environment. (The memorial would be built between the Washington and Lincoln memorials in Constitution Gardens, a grassy park in the National Mall that extends from the U.S. Capitol to the Washington Monument.)

Maya began to design the memorial right at the site. She didn't want to destroy the park in order to build a memorial there. Maya felt she had to use the landscape to add to the memorial's power, not take away from it. The memorial had to be a part of the park but also a private, special area.

She already had an idea from something she had seen at Yale. During Maya's freshman and sophomore years, the names of the Yale alumni who had died in the Vietnam War had been carved into a wall in Woolsey Concert Hall. As people walked by the wall, they could not only read the names of the dead but could also touch the names. Maya thought the idea of being able to touch the names on the Vietnam Memorial would be very powerful and emotional.

Maya saw the memorial as being part of the earth.

Maya Lin wanted visitors to the Vietnam Veterans Memorial to touch and be touched by the names of those who were killed or missing in action in the Vietnam War.

"It would be like walking into a shallow valley," Maya said. She pictured the earth opening up and a person being faced with two walls at an angle, carved with all the names of the dead. As people walked toward the memorial, they would have time to think and reflect. When they reached the wall, they could touch the carved names.

Maya returned to Yale and began working on her design. She sculpted a clay model of her idea to help her see it and then put her design on paper. The memorial would be made of polished black stone that formed a V-shaped wall. At the angle where the two sides of the wall would meet to form the V shape, the wall would be set down slightly into the ground. The names of the dead and missing people from the Vietnam War would be carved in gold lettering into the panels of the wall.

The group of eight judges for the contest was made up of architects, sculptors, and design specialists. They reviewed the entries for one week not knowing the names of any of the designers. After carefully looking at all the entries, the judges picked Maya's design. The judges said, "This is very much a memorial of our own times. The designer has created

The Vietnam Veterans Memorial, on the National Mall in Washington, D.C., is the most visited historical site in the nation's capital. It attracts more than 4 million visitors a year.

an eloquent place where the simple meeting of earth, sky, and remembered names contain messages for all who will know this place."

Almost as soon as the judges made their selection, however, there was criticism. Many people who had supported building a memorial did not like Maya's design, which came to be nicknamed "The Wall." Some of those opposed to it were veterans who had fought in the war. Others were so opposed to the design that they caused a lot of trouble and even tried to block the construction of the memorial.

Maya was personally attacked, too. The people opposed to her design said it looked like a "black gash of shame." She was accused of making a political statement about the war with her design of a black wall. Even racist and sexist comments were made. Some people said her design shouldn't be used because she was an Asian American, that the people who died in the war had been fighting Asians. Others said the designer should be a man, because mostly men had fought and died in the war.

Although there were people opposed to Maya's design, there were also many supporters of it. Most of the architecture and design world felt Maya's idea was brilliant. The Vietnam Veterans Memorial Fund committee also liked it, as did many people in Washington, D.C. But Maya was still very hurt by all of the negative things that were said about her design and about her personally.

This bronze statue, featuring three servicemen and an American flag, was added to the memorial, because some people felt that Maya Lin's design made an antiwar statement.

Disagreement over the memorial grew so strong that it looked like the memorial wouldn't be built. Finally a compromise was reached. A bronze statue of three servicemen, made by sculptor Frederick Hart, and an American flag would be placed near the wall as a part of the memorial.

Groundbreaking ceremonies for the wall were held on March 26, 1982, and construction began. By this time Maya had graduated cum laude (with distinction) from Yale in 1981. She decided to wait before starting graduate school at Harvard University so she could work as a consultant on the memorial.

During the building of the memorial, Maya faced more difficulties. Because she was not yet a licensed architect, and there were still many things that she did not know about construction, Maya had to work with an established architectural firm in the building of the monument. Some of the professionals she was working with tried to change her design. In another instance the memorial fund committee wanted the names of the dead to appear in alphabetical order. But Maya felt strongly that the names should be listed by date of death, following a chronological order.

Despite these setbacks, the completed memorial is beautiful and awesome. Each half of the wall is more than 245 feet long. The two sections are made up of 70 panels with more than 58,000 names carved into them. The highest point of the wall, where the two panels meet, stands more than 10 feet high, and the two sides taper out to a width of only 8 inches. The black stone is so highly polished that you can see your reflection in the panels.

Today people go to the memorial to find the names of friends and family members who died in Vietnam. They leave flowers, messages, and gifts. It is a place of peace, where people come to think and reflect, just as Maya had hoped it would be.

Her design for the Vietnam Veterans Memorial is considered to be a deeply moving piece of public art. It is the most visited historical site in the nation's capital, attracting more than 4 million visitors a year.

Four

"WORDS IN WATER"

Maya left Washington, D.C., in 1982 and started her graduate studies at Harvard University, in Cambridge, Massachusetts. But several months later, she dropped out of school. Not only was she still exhausted from the ordeal of building the memorial, now she was also a celebrity. Magazine and newspaper reporters called her constantly for interviews. She found it hard to be "Maya, the star designer." She wanted to go back to being just "Maya, the student" and get her master's degree in architecture.

She spent the summer teaching school at Phillips Exeter Academy in Exeter, New Hampshire. There she worked on her small art sculptures and took long bicycle rides. The summer renewed her, and in the fall she began graduate school at Yale. Maya had not liked Harvard, and she had decided to return to the school where she had earned her undergraduate degree.

The first year back at Yale was somewhat difficult

for Maya. She had to adjust to school again. Students and teachers still regarded her as a celebrity. Some people were jealous of how much she had been able to accomplish so early in her design career. Maya had begun to receive the first of many honors and awards, such as the Henry Bacon Memorial Award, a design award from the American Institute of Architects, given to her in 1984.

Soon things at school settled down, and she was able to get back into the routine of going to class and studying. After much hard work, including doing several projects for established architectural firms as well as taking her classes at Yale, Maya finally earned

After receiving a master's degree from the Yale School of Architecture in 1986, Maya Lin opened her own architecture and design studio in New York City.

The photo above shows the Peace Chapel at Juniata College in Huntingdon, Pennsylvania, where large stones form a circle for people to sit and meditate.

a master's degree in architecture in 1986.

After graduation Maya got her license in architecture and found some design projects. She worked on the **renovation** of a house in Connecticut, created a stage set in Philadelphia, and designed a small open-air gathering place, called the Peace Chapel, at Juniata College in Pennsylvania.

Drawing on her love of nature and the outdoors, Maya created an outdoor sculpture in Connecticut, called *Aligning Weeds*. She placed painted, aluminum rods in a streambed. The rods looked like living reeds.

In 1987 Maya moved to New York City. She found a loft space located in an area of the city where other artists lived. She set up her home and established her own architecture and design studio.

In the spring of 1988, Maya was contacted by an organization called the Southern Poverty Law Center, a legal organization located in Montgomery, Alabama. The head of the Southern Poverty Law Center asked if she would consider designing a monument for the organization.

The Southern Poverty Law Center, a nonprofit group founded in 1970 by lawyers Morris S. Dees and Joseph J. Levin, Jr., watches for and fights against racist and discriminatory activity. Discriminatory activity is unjust treatment of some people by others for unfair reasons. Morris Dees came up with an unusual legal plan to fight racists: filing lawsuits against the leaders of racist organizations to hold them financially accountable for their violent or illegal activities against people.

The Southern Poverty Law Center is also a place that contains information on the history of the Civil Rights Movement. During the 1950s and 1960s, this political movement had been organized to secure equal opportunity and treatment for members of minority groups. The movement sought to change laws, stop **segregation**, and give African Americans the right to vote in the South.

The people at the Southern Poverty Law Center told Maya that they wanted to build a memorial dedicated to the Civil Rights Movement and the people who died in it. Although there were several civil rights memorials in the United States, these were monuments to specific people. There was no memorial dedicated to the entire Civil Rights Movement and all the people who were involved and who died in the struggle. The Southern Poverty Law Center wanted a memorial that would honor these people and also be a tool of education. The memorial would be a record of the events that occurred in the long struggle.

The Southern Poverty Law Center sent Maya some videotapes and books about the civil rights era. She was too young to remember the civil rights era firsthand. Most of what she knew about the events and people from the movement came from history books and news reports. But Maya had experienced racism. When she was in Denmark during her junior year of college, Maya had gotten on a bus one day in Copenhagen. People had moved away from her after she sat down. It was the first time in her life that Maya had encountered discrimination, and it was an uncomfortable and embarrassing experience that she found hard to forget. When Maya won the Vietnam Veterans Memorial competition, racist comments about Maya's Asian-American background were made by some of the people who were opposed to her design. She has said that she found these comments disappointing and hurtful.

As she read the information sent to her, Maya learned that Montgomery, Alabama, where the memorial would be located, was the birthplace of the Civil Rights Movement. In 1955 Rosa Parks, an African-American woman, sat down in a Montgomery bus in a section that was reserved for white people only. The bus driver told her to move to the area in the back set apart for African Americans. (At that time in the South, it was a law that African Americans could sit only in specific sections on buses and other public transportation. This was known as segregated seating.) When Rosa Parks refused to give up her seat, the driver ordered her off the bus, and she was arrested.

After the incident the African Americans in Montgomery decided to boycott, or refuse to use, all public transportation. The boycott continued for 13 months, until Montgomery ended segregated seating

Many people participated in the struggle for racial justice, including Rosa Parks (right). She refused to give up her seat to a white person on a bus in Montgomery, Alabama, in 1955.

on its buses. This protest spread to other cities and to other aspects of segregation.

At the time the Reverend Dr. Martin Luther King, Jr., a young black minister, had been drawn into the bus boycott in Montgomery. He became the most famous and respected leader in the Civil Rights Movement, eventually winning a Nobel Peace Prize for his work. Dr. King inspired many other Americans to become involved in the fight for civil rights. Their struggle had continued through the 1950s and 1960s. The victories had been slow in coming. Finally the rights to sit where one pleased on public buses, to eat in restaurants, and to register to vote had been won.

The Reverend Dr. Martin Luther King, Jr. was the most famous leader of the Civil Rights Movement. Here he is seen delivering his "I Have a Dream" speech at the March on Washington, August 28, 1963.

But many people had died along the way. Some were famous, like Dr. King, while others were just ordinary citizens. The memorial would see that none of these people were forgotten.

Finally it was time for her to fly to Montgomery to look at the site planned for the memorial. On the plane Maya read a book about the Civil Rights Movement, called *Eyes on the Prize: America's Civil Rights Years, 1954–1965.*

In the book she came upon a passage:

"We will not be satisfied until justice rolls down like waters, and righteousness like a mighty stream."

The lines are from the Book of Amos in the Bible. Maya says that the minute she saw the quote she knew the memorial had to be about water. As she read further, Maya also discovered that Dr. King had used this same phrase not only in his famous "I Have a Dream" speech at the March on Washington in 1963, but also at the start of the bus boycott in Montgomery eight years earlier. So this phrase had been a kind of rallying cry for the entire Civil Rights Movement.

Maya thought about how the memorial could incorporate historical events, people's names, and the use of water in the design. A picture finally began to take shape in her head as the plane landed in Montgomery. A group of people from the Southern Poverty Law Center met her at the airport to take her out to lunch. By the time Maya got to the restaurant, she was able to sketch a rough design on a paper napkin for them. She saw the memorial as having a time line that listed both the major events of the movement and the individual deaths along the way. Together these two things would show how people's lives influenced history and how their deaths furthered the cause of civil rights. The words on the memorial would be carved in stone, and water would flow over the words.

In all, the names of forty people who died in the Civil Rights Movement were chosen to go on the memorial. The Southern Poverty Law Center wanted the memorial to be a representation of the sacrifices of all people, famous and ordinary, during the Civil Rights Movement. The memorial would record the events of the past but would also deal with the future. It had to show the continuing struggle for civil rights.

To accomplish both purposes, Maya saw the memorial as having two sections, both made of stone. As with the Vietnam Memorial, she chose black granite. The first part of the monument would be a 9-foot-high, 40-foot-long wall. On the face of the wall, carved in gold letters, would be the passage Maya had read in the book. Water would spill down the wall over the words. Maya decided to leave off the first part of the passage and start at the word "until." The carving would read:

...until justice rolls down like waters
    and righteousness like a mighty stream.
        —Martin Luther King, Jr.

..UNTIL JUSTICE ROLLS DOWN LIKE WATERS
AND RIGHTEOUSNESS LIKE A MIGHTY STREAM

MARTIN LUTHER KING JR

Maya Lin's design for the Southern Poverty Law Center's Civil Rights Memorial, honoring those who died in the Civil Rights Movement, was dedicated on November 5, 1989.

She felt that starting with the word "until" would tie in with one of the purposes of the monument, which was to show that the civil rights struggle still has a long way to go and must continue.

The second part of the memorial would be a 12-foot circular table resting on a pedestal at the base of the wall. On the surface would appear a time line of 53 events in the Civil Rights Movement (21 of them events that marked turning points in the movement) and the forty names of people who had died. The time line would be laid out like the face of a clock, and the carved words and names would be in gold letters. Maya planned to have water seep out from the table's center and flow over the names. This would invite people to touch them, thereby bringing some part of themselves to the memorial. The table would be only 31 inches high. She wanted it to be at a height that would make it easy for children to read.

Finally it was November 5, 1989, the day of the dedication. The Civil Rights Memorial was ready to be unveiled. Six hundred family members of the men, women, and children named on the memorial joined a crowd of 5,000 visitors, civil rights activists, and honored guests, such as Martin Luther King III. It

Maya Lin's design for the Civil Rights Memorial featured a time line of important events of the Civil Rights Movement.

was an emotional and inspiring day of songs, prayers, and speeches by survivors, such as Rosa Parks.

Maya looked out at the crowd of people from a window inside the Southern Poverty Law Center. "I like standing back quietly," Maya said. "You create your message, and then it is out there on its own." She felt this day was for the families and survivors of the Civil Rights Movement. Later, when she attended the official unveiling ceremony, Maya witnessed one of the most compelling and touching moments of the day. Rosa Parks, whose action on the bus 34 years before had helped set in motion the Civil Rights Movement, touched her name on the granite tabletop, and the water washed over her hands. Many people in the crowd started to cry.

Maya didn't anticipate the power that the words joined with water would generate. "I was surprised and moved when people started to cry," Maya said. Once again Maya had created a memorial that was both a historical record and a moving tribute. Her design had succeeded in honoring an important era and the people who had risked their lives for freedom in this country.

Chapter Five

ART AND ARCHITECTURE

As Maya was finishing work on the Civil Rights Memorial, she experienced sadness in her personal life with the death of her father. After she spent some time with her widowed mother, Maya returned to work on projects she had started while still doing the Civil Rights Memorial. She also had the first exhibitions of her small sculptures in art galleries. Her work was included in art shows in New York, California, and New Jersey. Maya said after the Civil Rights Memorial was completed that she was finished with designing large memorials. She had begun and ended the 1980 decade with historical memorials and was closing the door with a happy feeling on projects of this kind.

Her next public art project was an environmental piece in front of the Charlotte Coliseum in Charlotte, North Carolina. Maya worked together with a **landscape architect** named Henry Arnold. The pair were assigned to the project in 1989 and worked for two years, completing the piece in 1991.

Their design was composed of trees along a 60-foot-wide, grassy strip that leads up the middle of the driveway to the coliseum. On the strip of grass, Maya and Henry Arnold planted seven, ten-foot-wide juniper cypress trees. The trees were then trimmed into perfectly round shapes so they would resemble huge balls rolling across the grass. The effect is of balls being played in a game, like giant basketballs, imitating the actual sports events played in the coliseum. The artwork is called *Topo*, taken

Maya Lin's outdoor environmental sculpture, completed in 1991 and called *Topo*, adds a playful touch to the Charlotte Coliseum in Charlotte, North Carolina.

from the words "topography" (meaning natural features of land) and "topiary" (meaning the clipping or trimming of live shrubs or trees into decorative shapes).

Although she had said after the Civil Rights Memorial that she was through with historical memorials, Maya did create one more. In 1990 Yale University hired her to design a memorial detailing the history of female students at Yale. The university was founded in 1701, and for almost 300 years, it remained an all-male school. In 1969 the Yale graduate school opened its program to women, and finally Yale became a school for both men and women.

Maya loved the idea of a memorial piece celebrating

Maya Lin's tribute to the female students of Yale University, called *The Women's Table*, is outside the Sterling Memorial Library. The library is an important building on the undergraduate campus of Yale University.

the women at Yale. She used stone and water again to create a granite sculpture and water table. On the surface is another carved time line similar to the one on the Civil Rights Memorial. This time line, though, spirals out from the center of the table with numbers that represent the number of women students at Yale for each year of its existence. From 1701 until 1969 the only number is 0. It is a powerful visual reminder of how long women were denied entrance to the school. A bench in front invites people to sit by the piece. When it was completed in 1993, Maya named the work *The Women's Table*.

Much in demand Maya was juggling numerous other projects during this period. She designed the interior space for the new home of the Museum of African Art in New York City, by renovating two floors of an old loft building. Color is a major element of her design. Maya used subtle shades of color to suggest a passage through time as well as space. Color is used to link the different galleries. And she covered the walls of a meeting room with colorful fabric that was woven in Africa.

At the entrance Maya built a "forest" of tall copper pipes and copper mesh screens. Before the reopening of the museum in 1993, she worked side by side with the museum staff and a work crew to complete the interior. It is a quiet yet uplifting space.

In New York City, Maya also created her first sculpture involving moving parts. In 1988 an invitational design competition had been held by the Metropolitan Transportation Authority's Arts for Transit program to find two artworks for Pennsylvania Station, which was being renovated. Maya's design for an unusual clock was selected as one of the two pieces, and she was hired for the public art project.

Maya worked on this project for almost five years. She created a 38-foot-long clock that is designed to suggest a lunar eclipse. A lunar eclipse is when the moon passes through the shadow of the Earth cast by the sun. A large oval shape encloses a frosted-glass disk that is lit from a light source behind it. The numbers of the clock are etched on the disk. Moving back and forth on a track between the light source and the glass disk is an aluminum disk. The clock, titled *Eclipsed Time*, is permanently set in the ceiling above the ticket area of the Long Island Rail Road in Pennsylvania Station.

After the completion of *Eclipsed Time*, Maya was hired to create another piece of outdoor artwork. Her love of nature and the influence of the Ohio countryside really come through in this sculpture. *Groundswell* was made for the Wexner Center for the Arts in Columbus, Ohio, in 1993. It was the first time she had been asked to design something in her home state. The Wexner Center, designed by architect Peter Eisenman, opened at Ohio State University in 1989. The university wanted Maya to create an installation that would be a part of the very futuristic-looking

Maya Lin's sculpture *Eclipsed Time* was created in 1988 for New York's Pennsylvania Station and was one of two pieces selected in an invitational design competition.

building. It is five stories of unusual levels composed of steel tubes, brick, and concrete with huge windows made of smoked glass.

In thinking of a design, Maya recalled the mounds in Mound Builders State Memorial Park close to where she grew up. The Mound Builders were Native Americans who constructed earthen mounds during prehistoric times to serve as burial places, temples, and ceremonial earthworks.

Mysterious and beautiful to look at, the mounds make the earth look as if it is swelling up in the shapes of circles, rectangles, octagons (eight-sided shapes), and other forms. Maya said she had always been in

Maya Lin's *Groundswell* at the Wexner Center for the Arts in Columbus, Ohio. It was built to honor the Mound Builders, Native Americans who constructed earthen mounds to serve as burial places.

love with landscape and geology, and seeing these beautiful earth forms as a child must have had some influence on her.

Maya created a three-part sculpture of mounded glass "gardens" on different sites around the Wexner Center. Mixing clear and sea-green shattered glass, Maya piled up the glass like sand dunes and then "sculpted" the glass piles by combing them with a long, metal rake. The glass forms "gardens" of soft mounds. These mounds are similar in appearance to the ancient earthen mounds of Ohio as well as to rolling ocean waves and to Japanese raked-sand gardens.

With this artwork Maya was able to put her belief in recycling into practice. In the building of *Groundswell*, she used nearly 50 tons of recycled broken patio-door glass and safety glass from car windows that were donated by a commercial window recycler and the Ford Motor Company.

There was, however, one unhappy incident that spoiled this wonderful creative experience. A few months after *Groundswell* was completed, it was vandalized. Someone poured dry magenta paint pigment all over the largest of the three glass "gardens." The entire section of coated glass had to be thrown out and replaced with new glass. Maya went back to the Wexner Center and completely redid this part of the installation. She was hurt and angry that someone could be so cruel, especially in her home state. It was the only time any of her artwork had been purposely damaged.

But the destruction actually had a positive outcome. When Maya returned to fix her piece, instead of redoing it the way it had been before, Maya changed the design of this area. She ended up feeling that the new design was better than the original.

Chapter Six

IN TUNE
WITH NATURE

Maya's commitment to the environment is shown by the projects with which she is involved. Maya has agreed to design a proposed paper-recycling pulp mill in New York City's South Bronx, that would recycle tons of office paper from businesses. She also serves on a planning board that will advise the National Park Service on the best environmental uses for the former Presidio military base in San Francisco, California. Along with her public artwork, Maya has designed houses in California, Massachusetts, and Connecticut.

Maya's newest public sculpture is an outdoor piece completed in 1995. *Wave Field* is located at the University of Michigan, in Ann Arbor, Michigan. The outdoor sculpture is another example of the influence of Native American mounds and of the Ohio countryside. Maya designed a rectangular area of thick grass planted in wavelike mounds. Each mound is slightly different. Some are a little higher and

Maya Lin's *Wave Field*, at the University of Michigan in Ann Arbor, Michigan. Here students from the Department of Dance of the School of Music perform on the piece at its dedication on October 6, 1995.

others a little wider than the ones in front of them. Visitors often comment how the wave mounds appear to flow outward from the building entrances.

To Maya's surprise and delight, a documentary on her life and work was made by filmmaker Freida Lee Mock in 1994. The film is called *Maya Lin: A Strong, Clear Vision*, and it won an Academy Award in 1995 for Best Achievement in Feature Documentary.

Now in her late thirties, Maya is always on the go. She still lives in a loft in New York City, but now she also has a country house in Vermont. She likes to be alone and is a very private person. "My work is public, but I am not," she once said in an interview. Maya's

Maya Lin in her office. She prefers to work alone, late at night, with her cat (seen on Maya's worktable).

favorite time for working is not during the day at her office with staff around, but late at night with no one keeping her company but her pet cat.

Her long hair is gone, replaced by a shorter, simpler cut. But she still prefers to wear comfortable clothes, such as T-shirts and jeans, that suit her busy work style. For relaxation Maya would rather read or socialize with friends than watch television. Many of Maya's close friends and family are involved in the arts, too. Her boyfriend, for instance, is a sculptor, her mother is a writer, and her brother is a poet.

Over the years a number of people besides her parents have been an influence on Maya's life and work. At Yale she studied with Vincent Scully, a famous art and architecture historian, and Frank Gehry, a well-known architect. Vincent Scully, in particular, was very influential on Maya. He was her mentor at the School of Architecture. (A mentor is a person who counsels or guides someone.)

Another influence at Yale was the sculptor Ursula von Rydingsvard, from whom Maya took sculpture classes and who influenced the small sculptures Maya does now. Maya's large outdoor sculptures appear to have been inspired by artists such as Isamu Noguchi, Robert Smithson, and Richard Serra. She studied with Serra at Yale. All of these artists create sculptures of simple, bold forms and use natural materials, such as stone, in their work.

Maya still considers herself an artist whose work involves both architecture and sculpture. The challenge for her is to be labeled not as an architect or a sculptor, but as an artist who creates in both fields. "I love architecture, and I love sculpture, but I could never choose. Sculpture to me is like **poetry**, and architecture is like **prose**."

It is a good bet that an artist as talented as Maya Lin will never have to choose. With all that she has accomplished this early in her career, there are sure to be more exciting projects ahead for her in both architecture and sculpture.

1959   Born in Athens, Ohio, on October 5.

1977   Begins college at Yale University, in New Haven, Connecticut.

1981   Wins design competition for the Vietnam Veterans War Memorial. Graduates cum laude from Yale.

1984   Receives the Henry Bacon Memorial Award for Vietnam Veterans War Memorial from the American Institute of Architects.

1986   Receives master's degree in architecture from Yale.

1987   Receives honorary doctorate in fine arts from Yale.

1988   Creates *Eclipsed Time* in Pennsylvania Station, in New York City. Asked by Southern Poverty Law Center to design Civil Rights Memorial.

1989   Civil Rights Memorial completed. Creates *Topo* for the Charlotte Coliseum, in Charlotte, North Carolina.

1990   Commissioned by Yale University to design *The Women's Table* memorial artwork.

1992   Hired to design the interior space for the new home of the Museum of African Art, in New York City.

1993   Creates *Groundswell* in Columbus, Ohio.

1995   Creates *Wave Field* at the University of Michigan, in Ann Arbor, Michigan.

Glossary

Communism A social system in which all economic goods and property are owned by everyone in common.

landscape architect A person who plans and shapes outside spaces.

memorial Something that is intended to celebrate or honor the memory of a person or an event.

monument A structure, like a building or a sculpture, that is created as a memorial.

poetry An arrangement of words traditionally written or spoken in various patterns of rhyme, but not always.

prose Ordinary form of written or spoken words.

renovation To clean and repair a worn yard, house, or room.

segregation The act of separating from a main body or group.

Bibliography

Ashabranner, Brent. *Always to Remember: The Story of the Vietnam Memorial.* G.P. Putnam's Sons, 1988.

Isaacson, Phillip M. *Round Buildings, Square Buildings, & Buildings that Wiggle Like a Fish.* Alfred A. Knopf, 1988.

Levine, Ellen. *Freedom's Children.* G.P. Putnam's Sons, 1992.

Index